Alexa
The Ultimate User Guide to Use Alexa to the Fullest (Amazon Echo, Amazon Echo Dot, Amazon Echo Look, Amazon Echo Show, user manual, amazon echo app)

ROBERT FREEMAN

CONTENTS

Introduction

Amazon Echo is getting more powerful and smarter every week. Amazon is trying to make it a surprise package; therefore, they are constantly working on the expansion of their ecosystem with Echo Dot, Echo Look, Echo Show, and Amazon Tap. The main brain behind the device is Alexa—it powers your alarms/timers, smart home, music, and numerous other things. If you want to understand the capabilities of Amazon Echo devices, here are a few features of these devices:

A unique feature of the Alexa app, Echo Dot, and Amazon Echo is hands-free texting and calling. With the touchscreen of Echo Show, you can make video calls similar to FaceTime or Skype. You can block unwanted numbers for your convenience. A drop-in feature enables you to access any Echo device within your home, such as an intercom or Alexa app. To view the live feed in your room/home, you can pair Echo Show with your security cameras.

While receiving or placing calls, keep an eye on a light ring around your Echo device because it will turn green. If your text message or voice call is on the waiting list to be answered, the ring will turn yellow. After activation, these colors also work for future notifications. Setup for messaging or voice calling is easy because you will only have to grant access to your contact details through an app. It is just a start because you will get more features with Amazon Echo.

A premium member of Spotify can enjoy their favorite songs and playlists on the Amazon Echo. The integration of the device with Spotify is a plus of this global streaming platform. It bodes well for the expansion of Alexa from Amazon in the United Kingdom. It proves helpful to broaden the language knowledge of Echo beyond English because of the international status of Spotify. The premium users of Spotify can get a free trial for 30 days and the user of Amazon Echo can avail all these benefits.

The Alexa app is equipped with thousands of worthwhile and jaw-dropping skills. You use the advantage of Umber, Fitbit, and Domino's Pizza. Alexa can read trending tweets from Twitter. To get the advantage of the Alexa app, it is important to create an Amazon account and link your account with Echo devices through the Alexa app.

Some skills may not apply, so don't worry because there are numerous apps that work well with Alexa, such as noise apps, math puzzles, trivia, games, and numerous new additions. Alexa skills need your voice for activation. You can activate skills like smart home via your voice commands. For example, "Alexa, enable Fitbit."

It is quite easy to add new skills after having access to your Alexa app. You can manually search skills and add in your skill section. For improved results, you have to use a Skill Finder app to find out famous skills and use your voice to activate all of the appealing skills.

Chapter 1: Capabilities and Features of Amazon Echo

Initially, Echo was designed as a Bluetooth speaker and now it is equipped with advanced options. You can enjoy your favorite music with the use of Echo. If you don't want to pay monthly charges for Spotify premium, you can use the advantage of free music stores, such as TuneIn radio, iHeartRadio, and Pandora. Prime members of Amazon can get a huge collection of music with their annual subscription.

You can subscribe to music from Amazon to listen to millions of playlists and songs for only $3.99 per month on the Tap device, Echo, and Dot. To activate this monthly subscription, just ask Alexa to try unlimited Amazon music. New users will get a free trial for 30 days.

Listen to Kindle or Audiobooks

Audible can be an excellent way to listen to your favorite collection of audiobooks as a way to relax. Echo enables you to use the advantage of extra options, such as chapter selection and volume control. Kindle books are also available for Amazon Echo users and Alexa will help you search for your favorite books.

Multiple Alarms and Timers

Alexa is an ideal digital assistant for the bedroom and kitchen. You can purchase multiple Echos to increase their efficiency in your life. You can get the advantage of different features, such as setting customized alarms, multiple timers and alarms, and repeating alarms. You can easily set alarms to repeat regularly on particular weekdays or on a specific day.

Feel free to set timers and assign different names to timers, such as "Alexa, set meat timer for 20 minutes" that prove helpful in preparing meals. With a few simple features, you can make your life simple and beautiful.

Smart Home Skills for Thermostats, Switches, and Lights

The Amazon Echo enables you to create a smart home because a few devices can be integrated into smart products with Echo such as: thermostats (Sensi, Ecobee, and Nest), Caseta wireless lights (Lutron), Wemo and Philips Hue, Insteon and SmartThings, TP-LINK Kasa, LIFX, fans and lights (Haiku Home).

All smart home products are labelled under a skill tab as "Smart Home Skills" for easy management. You can see reviews of users before selecting a skill tab. Some smart products can be connected via third party in your Alexa app. Echo can control lights to make them dim or make them turn on and off. Amazon Echo is good to manage coffee makers, fans, heaters, and other smart things. Alexa is working to expand into vehicles and other smart home appliances.

Quick News Updates

Alexa offers essential news updates that are an excellent feature. You can start your morning without any extra hassle. You can control lots of news outlets with your voice, such as Discovery, BBC, NPR, CNN, and the Washington Post. You can also access AOL and NBC. Fox Sports and ESPN Radio are available to get headlines of your favorite games and sports stories. If you want to enjoy local news, there are more than a dozen municipal stations. You can view news of NBC 5 Chicago, NBC4 California, NBC 4 New York, and many others.

Sports Schedules and Scores

There is no need to wait for the news of your beloved team, because you have an option to receive updates of your teams. You can get quick outcomes of a game within a few seconds. You can ask about the time and date of a game. Echo offers you the most up-to-date information and knowledge of sports. You can instantly get live scores of your favorite match or game.

Updated Weather Forecast

You can get the latest updates about the current weather. This feature enables you to get the forecast of the weather for the next seven days. As you wake up in the morning, you will get the weather forecast from Alexa.

Prime Purchases and Tracking

Prime members of Amazon can enjoy numerous benefits. Prime members may avail two-day free shipping, cloud storage, free movies and videos, and free music. With Echo, you can re-order, order, and track packages made through Amazon. Alexa will inform you about the date at which the order was placed and expected time for the arrival of an order.

You can add a pin number that Alexa will inquire before re-ordering. It will create an essential layer of security. Non-prime items or add-on items can't be ordered, but Alexa may add these items to your shopping cart.

Shopping List through Alexa

It is nice to add something to your shopping list with your voice. The Amazon Echo can read the lists and you can feel free to add your required stuff. There is a problem that you can't clear any item or whole list with a voice command. You have to do this manually with the help of the Alexa app.

Play Movies with Alexa

With the use of a nifty feature, you can plan a special Friday night at the movies via straightforward commands. Alexa can inform you about nearby movies, times of movies in theaters, and movie information. After setting your location, you will get accurate news about movies. Once you get your desired movies, you can ask about actors, reviews, and ratings of movies. You can get times of movies for any impending date to plan ahead. It is easy for people to enjoy their favorite movies.

Event Calendar

You can link Alexa with a Google calendar. You can ask Alexa to add to your schedules, events, and forthcoming plans. It is an important tool for your business to increase the usefulness of Amazon Echo. You can get the advantage of "Quick Events" to add your favorite events. If Google is not connecting to your calendar, you can link to Microsoft Outlook, Apple iCloud, and Office 365.

Voice Recognition Far-Field

Amazon Alexa is better than Google Now, Cortana, and Siri because of its voice-recognition capabilities. It can recognize your voice from 10 to 15 feet. Alexa can successfully pick your voice and fulfill your demand.

Answer to Simple Questions

Amazon Echo is categorized as a special speaker with capabilities like Siri. You can ask questions to Alexa. The Echo offers spelling corrections, measurements, conversions, math calculations, Wikipedia, and intelligent answers.

Chapter 2: How to set up Amazon Echo in the UK

Amazon Echo is a great device that integrates with numerous third-party applications. You can set timers, alarms, or read calendar details, read news flashes, and play music with Alexa. It comes with numerous skills to increase your productivity. Users in the UK, Australia, and India need to follow different methods to set up Amazon Echo in their country.

If you want to set up Amazon Echo in the UK, you should follow this method correctly. You have to be careful because any mistake can affect how Amazon Echo works.

Install Alexa App

Users in the United Kingdom often face problems while trying to set up Echo. It is a fact that the Alexa app of Amazon (iOS, Android) is not available other than within the United States. Fortunately, you can solve this problem with the help of some simple instructions.

On Android

If you are using an Android device, the procedure will be really simple. Just install an APK file or install geo-restricted apps on your Android device. To install the Alexa app, you should have a VPN app to fake a location to your Google Play Store. You have to install a VPN app and manually select your location. You can install the Rocket VPN app available for free on the Play Store.

Open your selected VPN app and choose a country where the Alexa app is available, such as the United States. After selecting the United States, connect to a VPN service.

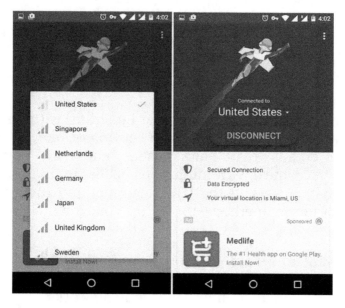

Now go to Settings > Apps > Google Play Store and hit "Storage." Move ahead and clear the cache data of your app. Now go back to the app info and tap "Force Stop."

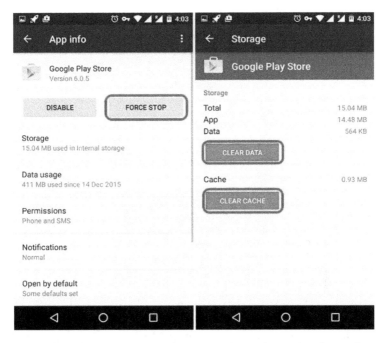

After doing this, you will move to Google Search and search for the Alexa app and hit the Play Store link for Alexa. If you try to search directly from the search functionality of the Play Store, you will not be able to find this app.

The link will direct you to the Play Store and you'll be able to see the "Install" button that was missing.

Now hit the "Install" button and Google will ask you to "Continue" setting up through your Play Store account. Choose "Skip" and the app will start downloading. You may have to keep your VPN apps running to use their advantage.

Change Time Zone

Echo is supported only in the United States and therefore it accepts locations and time zones within the US. If you want to get the advantage of smart home devices in the UK, you should use Echo without changing its time zone. Note that it will tell and display incorrect times and your reminders and alarms can't go off on the right time because of time zones. Its setting is quite difficult as compared to installing an Alexa app. You have to swindle with the requests of API. If you find it daunting, there is no need to worry. Here are step-by-step instructions for your convenience:

Get HTTP Request

Launch Chrome and explore alexa.amazon.com. Open the developer tools of Chrome (Command + Option + I on Mac) and circumnavigate to the "Network" tab.

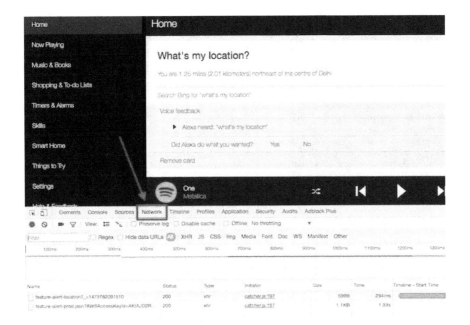

You have to type "device-preferences" in the Network tab's filter. You have to do this because you will see different HTTP requests with "device-preferences" in their own name that can be ones you desire to look out for.

In the website of Alexa, go to "Settings" and hit on the Echo. It may have a name something like ABC's Echo. Here, it is Sam's Echo.

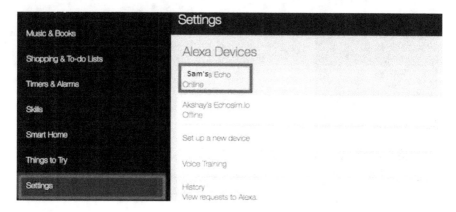

Scroll down and tap on "Edit" available next to the "Device Location."

Type a US-based address at this location and hit "Save." In the Tools of Developer, you can see some entries; choose a bottom entry. Now right-click on this option and choose "copy as cURL."

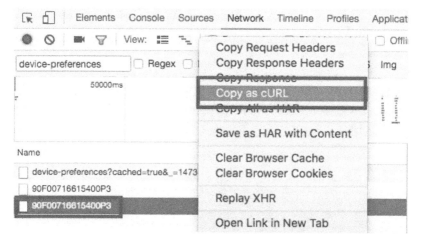

Play Around with This Request

You have to copy a request as a cURL and go ahead. Start changing the suitable values in the fields. Here are a few steps to get your time zone working on your Amazon Echo:

You have to paste the copied command in an editor like Notepad++ or Sublime Text. Now start editing the process. You have to change "timeZoneId" in the first place. Search for a "timeZoneID" in your text editor and paste a cURL command. Change it as per your time zone.

```
Address":null,"deviceAddressModel":{"city":"Seattle","countryCode":"US","c
"2201 Westlake Ave, Seattle, WA 98121, United States","postalCode":"98121"
Ave"},"deviceSerialNumber":"                    ","deviceType":"
us","notificationEarconEnabled"                            esponseStyle":
[],"temperatu                      "timeZoneId":'United Kindom     ' "voiceCastEnab
compressed
```

Once you are done, you have to make the following changes to reflect your values:

City: (United Kingdom)

Country Code: (UK)

Country: (write country name here)

District: (can be null)

House Number: (can be null)

```
CfM9ndaWMXd074="' -H 'Connection: keep-alive' --data-binary '{"deviceAccountId":"A3E
["city":"      l',"countryCode":    "county":null,"district":null,"houseNumber":null
ited States","postalCode":"98121","state":"WA","street":"Westlake
```

Now you can send a cURL request once again.

```
5b2Xq76LcGzq5EMZ8H+CfM9ndaWMXd074="' -H 'Connection: keep-alive' --data-binary '{"d
{"city":"     ","countryCode":"  ","county":null,"district":null,"houseNumber":null
:"98121","state":"WA","street":"Westlake Ave'},"deviceSerialNumber":"
```

If you don't have valid information for any field, you can simply use "null" values.

Once you are done with all settings, you can change values in the given fields:

- Set the "Postal Code" (there will be two codes; set the first one for your state).
- State: (UK or other state in the UK)
- Street (null or write value)

Send a cURL request once again.

Now update your second postal code and send a cURL command.

After doing this, you have to check the effects of your changes.

Send cURL Commands on Mac

It is easy to send cURL commands on a Mac. Macs come with pre-installed cURL. If you have a Mac, follow the given steps to send these commands:

- Copy a cURL request that you have to send.
- Open a Terminal and paste request, and finally tap Enter.

You are done with sending a cURL command on your Mac.

cURL Commands on Windows

You can send a cURL command on Windows and it is quite similar to sending one through a Mac. You have to download a cURL utility and install it before sending command. After installation, go to "Command Prompt, paste a cURL request and tap enter."

Check if all Changes Work

It is time to check if Amazon has accepted these changes. You can simply ask a question from Alexa like "Alexa, what is the time?"

If Alexa responds with the right time, then you have successfully changed the time zone.

Now ask, "Alexa, what is my location?"

Alexa tells your location in terms of distance from the middle of the city. This answer may have some fluctuation, but it should still work.

Now you are done with the basic functionality of your Amazon Echo to work for your location. You can ask Alexa to set reminders and alarms. These will work without any flaws.

Use Spotify with Echo

Spotify is an amazing streaming service for music that offers premium- and free-tiers for music. Unfortunately, Echo only needs premium membership. You can get started with Amazon Echo to stream music from your Spotify account.

Countries Available for Spotify

If you are living in a country where Spotify services are accessible, the setup can be really simple. You have to sign up for one premium account on your Spotify. It is free for the initial 30 days and then $9.99/month after 30 days. Just visit alexa.amazon.com and click on the "Books and Music" tab in the left menu. Select Spotify from the available list and log in with your Spotify account to initiate streaming music from Amazon Echo.

States without Spotify Support

If you are living in a state where Spotify is not available, you can work around that to stream music via your Amazon Echo from Spotify.

Install one VPN extension on your Chrome (select from available VPN extensions) and select "United States" as your country.

Now visit Spotify and tap on "Get Spotify Premium." You can start a free trial and fill up necessary sign-up details.

You have to provide your debit/credit card details. It may present another problem because you must have a credit/debit card of your selected country. They will not accept it so you have to fix this problem.

Virtual Debit Cards (Entropay)

You are finding it difficult to pay with the card of your own country. You can enter the Entropay website to get virtual VISA cards. These will be loaded with almost $5 cash and these can be ideal for you.

Just sign up on entropay.com and load cash in your VISA and virtual debit card. This debit card will work in the United States.

Now these will be helpful to sign up for music on Spotify and get a 30-day free trial of premium service. This card will be charged after your 30-day free trial. Make sure to have almost $10 in your Entropay credit/debit card. You can use Spotify as per your desire and cancel your subscription as per your convenience.

Differences of Alexa in the US and UK

Functionality of Spotify

You can activate your account after adding details of a valid card. On the Alexa website and app, you can log in with Spotify credentials. Now you can work with Alexa to play songs from Spotify.

Try saying, "Alexa, play *Hymn for the Weekend* by Coldplay from Spotify."

Alexa will inform you that it is streaming/playing *Hymn for the Weekend* by Coldplay from Spotify. It will start streaming the song as per your choice.

It is possible for you to play any song on Spotify. You can ask Alexa to play your favorite music.

Play Tracks from iTunes

You can play music from iTunes with the help of Amazon Echo. You can do it simply with the use of Amazon Echo. Just say "Alexa Pair" to put Amazon Echo in pairing mode. Open the Bluetooth settings on your iPhone and pair it with your Amazon Echo. You can listen to your favorite music on iTunes from Amazon Echo. The Echo can respond to your commands such as stop/pause/play, etc. You can easily control the playback of your music.

Use Nifty Tricks to Use Echo Outside of the United States

It is not good that Amazon Echo is not localized for lots of countries. You can make Amazon Echo functional in your own country like the United Kingdom. The only downside of this setting is that Alexa will not tell the weather of your area. You have to mention the name of the city in the command. Alarms, timers, and music streaming will not flawlessly work. There are lots of things to do with Amazon Echo. You can do neat tricks for small assistance. For this purpose, you will need smart accessories. You will read about these accessories later.

Chapter 3: Set up for Amazon Echo in the Accessible Areas of the UK

Users in the United Kingdom can activate Amazon Echo in their respective locations. Feel free to choose any location for set up, such as the kitchen counter, living room, bedroom nightstand, and other places where you want this voice-controlled device. You can use it without other devices enabled with Alexa. Before you start using your Echo and Alexa voice service, make sure to connect it to a Wi-Fi network and register it to your personal Amazon account through the Alexa app. For this purpose, follow the given steps:

Download the App and Sign in

The Alexa app is absolutely free and you can adjust this device to manage your shopping lists, music, alarms and many other things. You can download the Alexa app on your Android 4.0+ devices, iOS 7.0+ devices, and 2.0+ Fire tablets. You can download the Alexa app from the Apple,

Amazon, or Google Play app stores. If you want this app for your computer with Wi-Fi, you can visit https://alexa.amazon.co.uk

First- and second-generation Kindle Fires, second-generation Kindle Fire HD 7" and Fire HD 8.9" tablets don't support the Alexa app.

Amazon Echo Activation in the UK

Select a central location for your Amazon Echo, such as a place that should be 8" away from windows and walls. Plug the integrated power adapter in your Amazon Echo and finally plug in your power outlet. See the light ring turn blue and then orange. As the light color turns to orange, Alexa will greet you. Keep in mind that other phone chargers and USB adapters may not work well to provide sufficient power to your Amazon Echo.

Wi-Fi Network Connection

Feel free to connect to your Wi-Fi app with the help of on-screen instructions. Sometimes the setup procedure may not start automatically; therefore, you can press Wi-Fi or the Bluetooth button and hold it for a few seconds. You will get the Alexa app and can easily explore settings and start set up for your new device.

How to connect your Wi-Fi?

Amazon Echo in the United Kingdom can connect with private and public Wi-Fi networks and hotspots. Echo can't connect to ad-hoc networks. Follow the given instructions:

- You have to access the left-navigation panel and select "Settings."

- In the settings, you can select your device and update Wi-Fi.

If you want to add a new device to your Amazon account, you will hit "Set up a new device."

Now press and hold the Wi-Fi button to let the light turn orange. You can connect your mobile device and list of other networks to your Amazon Echo. Alexa may instruct you to manually connect your particular device to Amazon Echo with the help of Wi-Fi settings.

Select your Wi-Fi network and enter a password for your network to secure it. If your network is not available, you can add your network manually or rescan it. If you have trouble with the Wi-Fi setting, you can reset your Echo device to its factory setting.

A Secure and Reliable Wi-Fi Connection

You can connect your device to a Wi-Fi network. The following are some instructions to connect your Amazon Echo through Wi-Fi:

- In the first step, plug your Echo in the outlet and browse the Amazon Echo app on your phone or computer. The Echo will connect to the dual-band Wi-Fi networks 2.4 Ghz–5Ghz. Keep in mind that ad-hoc networks are not supported by Echo.

- Open the navigation panel of the Echo app and then go to "Settings" and access name of your Echo. You have to update your Wi-Fi. If you are setting it for the first time or want to add a new Echo in the account, you can hit "Set up a new Echo." Keep in mind that you can change the Wi-Fi network anytime in the Echo app.

- There is an action button on your Amazon Echo; just hold it for five seconds and see the light ring change to orange. Your mobile device will be connected to the Amazon Echo and you can check the list of available networks in the app.

- Select your own Wi-Fi network and enter a password, and then hit "Connect." If your network is not available in the list, then you can scroll down to add your own network. You can add a network manually in the Echo App to connect your device to the network.

You will get a confirmation message in the app confirming the connection of Echo with your Wi-Fi network. Now return to the home screen of your app to start using Echo.

Communicate with Alexa

The Amazon Echo is available for your use, and to activate it, you need to say the "wake" word. You can start speaking naturally into your device because after listening to the wake word, the device will start working.

You can now speak to your device by calling it "Alexa." You can change this name to "Amazon" anytime in the app. In the app, go to the setting and select "Wake Word" and then make the necessary changes.

Solve Different Problems with a Reset Command

Numerous times, you can manage different problems of Amazon Echo by resetting it. Before resetting your device, it will be good to restart it to see if it is useful. If the problem still persists, then you can reset the Amazon Echo:

- Use a paper clip to press the reset button for five seconds. The button is located at the base of the device near the power adapter port. When you reset the device, the light ring will turn from blue to orange.

- Wait for some time to let the light ring turn off and on once again. The light ring turns blue and goes into setup mode.

- Open the app to connect your device to a Wi-Fi network and register it to your existing Amazon account. It is time to follow the whole setup procedure once again to configure your device.

Portable Alexa is available on Echo and to speak to your Alexa, you have to hit the microphone button and speak in a natural voice. Try to speak short and natural phrases and put your Echo in sleep mode to save battery life.

Charging Instructions for Echo

A micro-USB cable, charging cradle, and power adapter is available with Amazon Echo. Your device will require four hours to charge. Fully charged Amazon Echo can continue working for almost nine hours. Follow these instructions:

- Use the charging cradle to securely place your Amazon Echo.

- Connect one end of the cable to the charging cradle and the other end should be connected to a power adapter.

- Plug this adapter into your power outlet and check that the power button is glowing.

- You can check the current battery level of Amazon Echo by asking Alexa about battery percentage or use the Alexa app to see the battery percentage in the menu. Playback controls will also help you check the battery percentage.

Replicating Alarms with Alexa

It is easy to adjust alarms with Alexa for one day, two days, one week, or on a regular basis. You can use voice commands such as:

"Alexa, set an alarm for Tuesdays at 8 p.m."

"Alexa, set the alarm for every Monday at 6 a.m."

Amazon Echo

Amazon Echo utilizes far-field technology to recognize your voice. It is easy to give a command to Alexa from another room. You can directly connect to Echo via an audio cable or Bluetooth. Make it easy by adding voice control to the stereo system of your home. Its built-in speaker will help you keep the Echo in your bedroom and set a smart timer to turn lights on and off. Set timers in the kitchen and add items to your shopping list with the help of Echo.

Simple to Set Up and Easy to Use

Amazon Echo can connect to your home Wi-Fi or mobile hotspot. The Alexa app is available for your iOS, Android, and Fire devices. There are a few quick steps that will help you start your Echo:

- Turn on your Amazon Echo.

- Connect to the internet with the Alexa app

- With Echo, you can ask for weather, music, news, and much more

Voice Recognition Training

It is important to enhance your experience because the training helps Amazon Echo to recognize your speech in a better way. You have to speak 25 phrases and it will take only a few minutes to complete. It will not be displayed in the dialogue history. The following are some tips for the voice training:

- Once the Echo ring turns red, you can hold the microphone button to activate microphones.

- Select a place where you will normally speak to the Amazon Echo. Speak normally to your Echo and say every phrase that you will use.

- If you have a remote, then keep it away during voice training.

Learn About the Home Screen

The home screen card contains some useful actions that are taken recently by you. It may contain:

- A description of your current activities

- Options for contents similar to your search results

- Link to the web to collect more information

- Options for voice feedback to enhance your experience

- Improve your voice recognition

- Remove the card

Learn How to Start Voice Training

- Open the left-navigation panel and hit "Voice Training" then select "Start."

- Speak normally and then select "Next." If you want to repeat a phrase, hit "Pause and then repeat the phrase."

- After completing your session, go to the home page and end your session at any time. You can also pause the session before ending it.

You can explore your transcripts and listen to the recorded interaction with your Amazon Echo. It is also possible to delete the specific recording. Following are some steps that will help you to hear your dialogue history:

- Open settings from the navigation panel

- Select the "Dialogue History"

- Hit the play icon and start listening to a specific recording

You can select any individual recording to delete it and remove the audio streaming file from the cloud and home screen cards.

Delete Your History

You can delete all of your recorded interactions with the help of your Amazon Echo app:

- Go to an option given for the management of your devices and other contents, and then hit "Your Devices" tab.

- Check the list of devices in your Amazon account and select your Amazon Echo.

- Open the "Device Actions" in the dropdown menu and then select "Manage Voice Recordings."

- Select delete to remove all interactions.

The Echo will understand your voice commands and it is better than any other portable speaker. It can accept your voice commands, offer voice controls, and Wi-Fi streaming. It is designed to be moved to the park and play your favorite music at a party. It is perfectly portable and easy to clip to your bag.

Chapter 4: Apps to Use with Amazon Echo

Amazon Echo is designed to make your life smart. There are numerous apps to incorporate with Alexa. These are good to add to Amazon Echo through Alexa. If you can access Alexa, you can use the advantage of different apps.

Capital One

Capital One will increase the capabilities of Alexa because you can pay bills with your device. You can link your device with Capital One credit and debit cards via the Alexa app and you can ask for different updates, such as card balance, money in your account, and details of recent transactions. Capital One will help you transfer money easily.

Automatic Apps

These skills are excellent to add into your Alexa without any additional hardware. This will be a clever integration in your device because you can automate your accounts and ask all sorts of questions from your Amazon Tap. For instance, you can ask about your driving performance, destinations of kids in your car, and your current location. You can ask your fuel level and other details regarding your car. It will be a great addition to your smartphone to plan your journey.

Domino's Pizza

Amazon Tap's Domino skill will help you turn your wish into a yummy reality. You can order a pizza by creating a link between the Alexa app and your Domino's account. After this, it will be really easy for you to get delivery on a whim. It is really easy to order your favorite pie and get it at your door. You only have to say "Alexa, open Domino's to place my special/easy order." You can also ask for a status update on your delivery from your Amazon Tap.

Quick Events

You can add quick events to your Google calendar in a hurry on your Android and iPhone with the help of their touchscreens. Try swiping and tapping quick events with the help of a spontaneous scheduling skill. You can enter your information and Alexa will tell you about the appointments and events for the next day. Update your calendar on a regular basis to enhance your productivity and get rid of the tensions of your busy life.

Jeopardy

Jeopardy is a delightful surprise in the Amazon Tap as it helps you play your favorite entertaining show. You can flex your knowledge with six new questions on a regular basis. You can select multiple categories to improve your knowledge.

Spelling Bee

Amazon Tap can be used cleverly with the help of the Spelling Bee. This is a simple app that will help you improve your knowledge. It can recite words that a user has to speak loudly. Tap knows the spelling of these words and the Tap will act as the referee. It is an excellent choice for a quick mental exercise or to get ready for a competition. It will be a fun and knowledgeable way to pass your time.

NBC News

The election is a hot topic for everyone and you can learn about ballots with the help of NBC News. This will help you get polling data, initial results, latest headlines, trivia, and discussion of pundits. You can get all the important news and highlights automatically instead of designating a special time to listen to the news.

Wayne Investigation

Regardless of your views about Batman, you can activate this skill on your Tap platform to get its full potential. You can select an audio-based and high-quality adventure game. It is designed for fun and you can assume the role of an investigator to have some fun. You can discover a murder and the narrator will tell a story with excellent sound effects. It is an excellent way to explore Gotham in a new way.

Uber

If you are looking for a personal assistant, the Tap can help you get a car. You can use Uber skills and Alexa will find out your credentials from your account. You have to add your location in the app and ask Uber to get a car. You can ask about traffic, status of the car, and change the order of your car.

7-Minute Workout

If you want to improve your health and always wanted to be healthy, you should follow a set of particular exercises. This app has some exercises that are scientifically proven for your health. The Tap will become your trainer and you can follow a workout routine. Amazon Tap will record your efficiency and track the statistics. With the passage of time, you will get difficult exercises.

Chapter 5: How to use Echo Show and Echo Look

Echo Look enables you to take full-length photographs of your regular look with the help of your voice. With its depth-sensing camera and built-in LED lighting, you can blur your background to pop your outfit. You will get shareable and clean photographs. Get a live view in your Look app or request Alexa to take a video to see yourself from different angles. You can check recommendations based on your regular look and use a style check to use as a second opinion. Alexa is designed in the cloud and she is really smart and getting smarter day by day. It is a hands-free camera to analyze your whole look.

Check Your Style from Different Angles

Take short videos or full-length photographs, so that you can take a 360-degree view of an outfit. You can use this app to create your own lookbook. Use vision-based computer background blur to pop your outfits.

Introduce Style Check

With the Style Check app, you can get the advantage of cutting-edge machine-learning algorithms and get advice from fashion experts. Submit two photographs to get a second opinion on your outfit based on current trends, styling, color, and fitting. These inputs and feedbacks from fashion experts can help you make smart decisions.

Always Work Smartly

You can instruct Alexa to read audiobooks, news, weather updates, and much more. Get ready for an easy day and ask Alexa to access your calendar, check the commute, and order one latte from Starbucks. Alexa is becoming smarter day by day and new skills can make your work easier.

Amazon Echo Show

Simple to Set Up & Use

1. Plug in Echo Show

2. Connect to the internet using Echo Show

3. Just ask for music, weather, news, and more

It is a new visual aid in the Alexa-enabled products. With the help of Echo Show, you can see items before purchasing them. Echo Show is a good extension for users of Amazon Echo, Dot, and Tap. It is another member of the Echo family. It comes with a camera and a screen so you can see the results of video chats and queries.

Echo Show is publicly available for sale. You can purchase a 7-inch touchscreen device in white or black for $229. The Prime members of Amazon can get it within two days. The Amazon Echo Show is a speaker and screen device to improve the performance of Alexa. It helps you watch movies, play music, control smart gadgets, and video chat with family and friends.

It sports a 7-inch touch-sensitive screen and two front-facing Dolby speakers and eight microphones. It can easily hear your query from anywhere in the room, even while you are watching a video or listening to music. The Show has a front-facing 5MP camera to make video calls to your family and friends with Echo Show. With the help of the Alexa app, you can play videos on your iPad or iPhone.

echo show

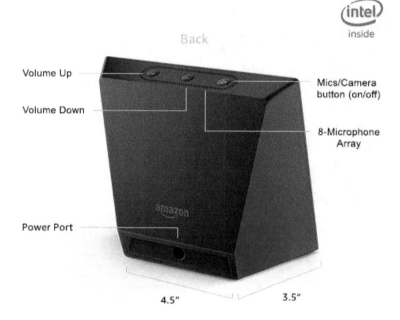

Front

Front Facing Camera

7"

7.4"

7.4"

intel
inside

Back

Volume Up

Volume Down

Mics/Camera
button (on/off)

8-Microphone
Array

Power Port

amazon

4.5"   3.5"

Conclusion

Amazon Echo is an advanced speaker with a virtual assistant called Alexa. You can control this speaker with your voice, receive messages, send messages, make calls, play music, and listen to the news, sports scores, and weather updates.

Echo comes with forming technology beam and seven microphones. Echo is an advanced speaker to help fill your room with immersive 360-degree sound. You can instantly activate Amazon Echo with only a "wake" word.

Thank you for reading. I hope you enjoy it. I ask you to leave your honest feedback.

I think next books will also be interesting for you:

Amazon Echo

Amazon Echo Guide

Amazon Echo Dot

Amazon Echo Dot

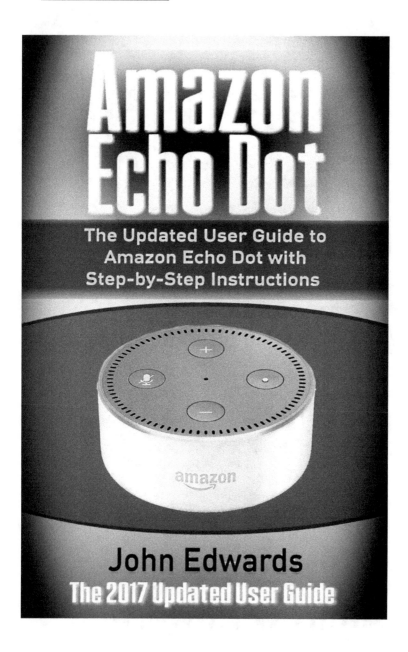

Kindle Fire HD

Kindle Fire HD
8 & 10
The Ultimate User Guide to Master Your Kindle Fire HD

Alex Cooper